CW00421610

Voiceplay

Songs by Alison Street and Linda Bance

Illustrated by Laure Fournier

MUSIC DEPARTMENT

OXFORD
UNIVERSITY PRESS

Copy kitten

Copy kitten, copy kitten,
miaow, miaow, hiss!
Copy kitten, copy kitten,
sounds like this!

Sit by me

If you want to sing a song,
sing a song, sing a song.
If you want to sing a song,
sit by me.

If you want to play a drum,
play a drum, play a drum.
If you want to play a drum,
sit by me.

What shall I find?

What shall I find in my birthday present?
What shall I find in my birthday present?
What shall I find in my birthday present?
Early in the morning.

Let's all play with my birthday present,
let's all play with my birthday present,
let's all play with my birthday present,
early in the morning.

Barney Bear

Barney Bear is walking,
walking, walking.
Barney Bear is walking,
walking to the park.

Barney Bear has found a friend,
Barney Bear has found a friend,
Barney Bear has found a friend,
going to the park.

Sally go round the sun

Sally go round the sun,
Sally go round the moon,
Sally go round the chimney pot
on a Thursday afternoon. *Boom*!

On a log

On a log, Mister Frog,
sang his song the whole day long,
glumf, glumf, glumf, glumf!

In a pen, Missus Hen,
clucked around and scratched the ground,
squawk, squawk, squawk, squawk!

In a hole, Mister Mole,
curled up tight and slept 'til night,
snore, snore, snore, snore!

Five icicles

Five icicles, five icicles,
five icicles hanging around.
One melted—*mm*!

Under the cover

I am hiding under the cover,
under the cover, under the cover.
I am hiding under the cover,
guess how I will be?

I'll be very, very happy,
very, very happy,
that's how I will be!

Lula's lullaby

Rock-a-by, lullaby,
my baby sleep-a-by.
Stars in the sky-a-by,
twinkle goodnight.

Rock-a-by, lullaby,
why do you cry-a-by?
I love you so, and I
kiss you goodnight.

Gingerbread Man

Run, run, run,
as fast as you can,
you can't catch me
I'm the Gingerbread Man.
Little old woman and little old man,
you can't catch me
I'm the Gingerbread Man!

The wolf's tale

I'm a big, bad wolf,
my name is Keith,
I'll tell you my adventures.
I huffed and I puffed 'til I blew out my teeth
and I had to get new dentures.
So now I cannot huff,
and now I cannot puff,
I am no longer snappy.
I moved in with the little pigs,
and we're really, really, really, really happy!